A Prayerful Path to Peace:

A Guide to Spiritual Growth in 2023

Mathew C. Johansson

TABLE OF CONTENTS

Introduction

The idea of a prayerful path has become increasingly popular in recent years as people seek to bring more spiritual guidance and connection into their daily lives. A prayerful path is a way of life that focuses on prayer and meditation as tools to deepen one's connection to God. It is a path of faith that leads to a deeper understanding of the Creator and the world around us. At its core, the prayerful path is an effort to bring the power of prayer into our lives. By focusing on prayer and meditation, we can begin to understand our relationship with God and learn how to better serve Him. This can lead to a more meaningful connection with God, helping us to grow in our understanding of His will and how to live in accordance with it. The prayerful path is not a one-size-fits-all approach to spiritual growth, however. It is an individualized journey that requires thought, reflection, and dedication. By establishing regular prayer and meditation practices, individuals can gain greater insight into their own spiritual needs and desires, which in turn can lead to a more fulfilling spiritual life.

For those just beginning to explore the prayerful path, it is important to remember that it is a lifelong journey. Taking the time to explore your own relationship with God can be a rewarding experience, but it is important to take it one step at a time. When starting out, it can be helpful to establish a routine of daily prayer and meditation, as well as to explore different forms of spiritual practice and guidance. The prayerful path is an opportunity to deepen one's connection with God and to gain a better understanding of the mysteries of life. It is an individual journey that can lead to a more meaningful spiritual life and a greater sense of peace and fulfillment. No matter where you are in your spiritual journey, the prayerful path can offer insight and guidance.

As we face a new year and a world full of uncertainty, it is more important now than ever to take time for ourselves and focus on our spiritual growth. A Prayerful Path to Peace is designed to help you do just that. This guide will provide you with simple, effective strategies to help you create a peaceful, prayerful space in your life.

It will provide guidance on how to cultivate a more mindful, prayerful mindset and how to connect with your spiritual self. You will also learn how to access your inner strength and courage so that you can face your worries and anxieties with a prayerful attitude. The guide includes many different exercises and activities to help you develop your own unique prayerful practice. You will learn how to establish a regular prayerful practice that is tailored to your individual needs. At the end of this guide, you will have the tools necessary to create a powerful and meaningful prayerful practice. You will be able to use your practice to bring greater peace and joy into your life and the lives of those around you. We hope that you find this guide to be helpful and inspiring. We hope your new year is peaceful and prosperous

Chapter 1

Growing in Faith

Growing in faith is an incredibly important part of any spiritual journey. It is a process of questioning, learning, and deepening our faith in God and His Word. As we grow in faith, our relationship with God is strengthened and our understanding of His Word deepens. The path to a meaningful and fulfilling life is often found in prayer and the study of the Bible. A Prayerful Path is a journey of faith that involves taking time to reflect and draw nearer to God through prayer, meditation, and study of the Bible. This path is all about using the Bible to help us gain a better understanding of God's will and purpose for our lives. The Bible is filled with powerful and encouraging passages that remind us of God's promises and grace. By regularly reading and reflecting on scripture, we can gain insight and wisdom to help us live a life that is pleasing to God. We can also learn how to walk in faith, trusting in God's plan for us and leaning on Him for strength and guidance.

Growing in faith is one of the most important aspects of being a Christian. It is the foundation of our relationship with God, and it is what allows us to access His power, His grace, and His love. The Bible is the ultimate source of knowledge and guidance when it comes to growing in faith. It contains many verses and chapters that are specifically written to help us understand how to live a life of faith and trust in God. One of the most important aspects of growing in faith is to spend time in the Word of God. The Bible contains many passages that are specifically written to encourage us to have faith and trust in God. For example, Romans 10:17 says, "*So then faith comes by hearing, and hearing by the word of God.*" This verse teaches us that faith comes from hearing God's Word, so it is important to spend time reading the Bible and studying the Scriptures. We can also grow in faith by praying and trusting in God. In 1 Thessalonians 5:17, it says, "*Pray without ceasing.*" This verse teaches us that we should be in constant communication with God through prayer. We should be praying for guidance, strength, and direction, and we should be trusting in God's will and His plan for our lives.

It is also important to practice obedience to God's commands. In 1 John 3:22-23, it says, "*And whatever we ask we receive from Him because we keep His commandments and do those things that are pleasing in His sight.*" This verse teaches us that we should be obedient to God's commandments in order to receive the blessings and abundance He has promised to those who follow Him. Finally, we should be spending time with other believers. In Hebrews 10:24-25 it says, "*And let us consider one another in order to stir up love and good works, not forsaking the assembling of ourselves together, as is the manner of some, but exhorting one another, and so much the more as you see the day approaching.*" According to what this verse teaches, we should associate with other believers in order to encourage each other and to build one another up in the faith. Growing in faith is a journey that requires dedication, effort, and time. However, the rewards are plentiful. Through reading the Bible, praying, obeying God's commands, and spending time with other believers, we can develop a faith that will carry us through life's storms and into eternity.

How can I grow in faith?

1. Pray for a stronger faith. (Psalm 37:4)

2. Read the Bible regularly. (2 Timothy 3:16)

3. Spend time in worship and prayer. (Psalm 95:2)

4. Serve others. (Mark 10:45)

5. Surround yourself with other believers. (Hebrews 10:23)

6. Meditate on God's promises. (Psalm 16:8)

7. Attend church and fellowship with other believers. (Hebrews 10:24-25)

8. Obey God's commands. (John 14:15)

9. Spend time in silence. (Psalm 46:10)

10. Trust in God. (Proverbs 3:5-6)

Chapter 2

Cultivating Gratitude

Gratitude is a strong feeling that has the potential to significantly impact our lives. It can improve our relationships, increase our happiness, and help us to have a more positive outlook on life. Gratitude is an attitude of thankfulness and appreciation for the blessings we have in life. It is a powerful emotion that can bring peace, joy, and contentment to our lives. Cultivating gratitude to God is an important practice for Christians, as it helps to bring us closer to Him and allows us to show our appreciation for all that He has done for us. It can also help us to stay focused on the many blessings that we have in our lives and to remember that God is always with us, even in difficult times. There are many ways to cultivate gratitude to God. First, it is important to be mindful of the blessings that God has given you. This can be done by regularly reflecting on the good in your life and thanking God for it. You can also take time out of each day to give thanks to God for the blessings He has bestowed upon you.

This can be done through prayer or simply by saying a prayer of thanks when you wake up in the morning or before you go to bed at night. It is also important to be aware of the spiritual gifts that God has given you. Recognizing the gifts that He has bestowed upon you and being thankful for them can help to cultivate a deeper appreciation for all that He has done for you. You can also take time to study scripture and read the stories of the Bible, which can help to remind you of all the ways God has been faithful to you. Finally, it is important to show gratitude for God's love and grace in your everyday life. This can be done through acts of service, such as helping your neighbor or volunteering at a local charity. It can also be done through acts of kindness, such as sending a card or making a donation to a charity in need. Whenever you do something kind or generous, take a moment to thank God for His love and grace. Cultivating gratitude to God is an important practice that can help to strengthen your relationship with Him and bring peace, joy, and contentment to your life.

Taking time to thank Him for all that He has done for you and being mindful of the blessings He has bestowed upon you can help to bring you closer to Him and remind you of all the ways He has been faithful to you.

How to cultivate gratitude

Read and meditate on the following scriptures and practice gratitude:

1. *Give thanks to the Lord for He is good and His love endures forever* (Psalm 106:1).
2. *Enter His gates with thanksgiving and His courts with praise* (Psalm 100:4).
3. *Give thanks in all circumstances; for this is God's will for you in Christ Jesus* (1 Thessalonians 5:18).
4. *Rejoice always, pray continually, and give thanks in all circumstances* (1 Thessalonians 5:16-18).

5. *For everything God created is good, and nothing is to be rejected if it is received with thanksgiving* (1 Timothy 4:4).

6. *Sing to the Lord, give thanks to his name; make known among the nations what he has done* (Psalm 105:1).

7. *Give thanks to the Lord, for he is good; his love endures forever* (Psalm 136:1).

8. *Devote yourselves to prayer, being watchful and thankful* (Colossians 4:2).

9. *Let us come before him with thanksgiving and extol him with music and song* (Psalm 95:2).

10. *Let them give thanks to the Lord for his unfailing love and his wonderful deeds for mankind* (Psalm 107:8).

Chapter 3

Developing Compassion

Developing compassion for the things of God can be a challenging task. It requires a great deal of dedication, patience, and understanding. It also requires a willingness to be open to God's will and to learn about His ways. Compassion is a beautiful thing, and it will open up a world of possibilities for those who choose to dedicate themselves to it. The first step to developing compassion for the things of God is to take the time to learn about Him. This can be done by reading the Bible, attending church services, and talking to others who share your faith. By learning more about God, His teachings, and His plans, you will begin to understand His character and His will. You will also gain an appreciation for the things He has done and is doing. Once you have a better understanding of God, the next step is to practice showing compassion. This can be done through acts of kindness, such as volunteering at a local church or helping those in need.

It is also possible to accomplish this through prayer and meditation. Taking time to reflect on God's goodness and to practice gratitude for the blessings He has given can be a great way to show your love and appreciation for Him. Finally, it is important to remember that developing compassion for the things of God is a lifelong journey. It is not something that can be achieved overnight. It takes time and effort to cultivate true compassion, but the rewards are worth it. With patience, dedication, and a willingness to learn, anyone can develop a deep and loving relationship with God.

Developing compassion in a prayerful path to peace is an important journey we can all take. Compassion is a powerful emotion that allows us to empathize with others and understand the difficulties they are going through. It is a source of strength, a keystone for understanding, and a source of inspiration for us to reach out and help others. In a prayerful path to peace, compassion is a key ingredient for creating a harmonious life.

How do I develop compassion for the things of God?

1. Pray for an open heart and mind. (Psalm 51:10)
2. Meditate on the Bible. (Philippians 4:8)
3. Ask God to help you see others with compassion. (Matthew 5:7)
4. Pray for courage to serve others in need. (Matthew 25:40)
5. Ask God to remove feelings of judgment and prejudice. (Romans 12:15)
6. Pray for humility and patience. (Colossians 3:12-13)
7. Ask the Holy Spirit to fill you with compassion. (1 John 4:7-8)
8. Pray for strength to love your enemies. (Luke 6:27-28)
9. Ask God to give you a compassionate heart. (Psalm 51:17)
10. Pray for patience and understanding. (Galatians 6:1-2)

Chapter 4

Living in Service

Living in service to God is a privilege and a blessing. It is a way to show your devotion and faith in the Lord and to recognize the power and grace of His Spirit. Living in service to God can be challenging, but with time and dedication, it can be done.

The first step to living in service to God is to develop a strong relationship with Him. This means reading His word and studying the Bible so that you can gain insight into His will and His ways. Prayer is essential to this process as it allows you to communicate your needs, concerns, and desires to the Lord. As you do this, you will begin to find yourself drawn closer to Him and His will.

The second step to living in service to God is to set yourself apart from the world. This means abstaining from any behavior that is not in line with His teachings. This includes avoiding gossip, dishonesty, and any form of idolatry.

It also means being aware of the things that you consume, such as television, movies, and video games, and making sure that they are in line with God's values.

The third step to living in service to God is to serve others. This means being generous with your time, energy, and resources. God calls us to serve our fellow man, and this can be done in a variety of ways. Volunteering at a soup kitchen, helping out a friend in need, or simply offering a listening ear and words of encouragement are all great ways to serve others in His name.

The fourth step to living in service to God is to stay in fellowship with other believers. This means attending church, Bible study, and other Christian gatherings. It also means making sure that you are surrounded by like-minded individuals who will encourage and challenge you to live a life that is pleasing to God.

Finally, the fifth step to living in service to God is to stay humble and remember that you are not perfect. This means recognizing that you will make mistakes and that you are not always going to have the answers.

It also means learning to accept constructive criticism and seeking out advice and guidance from those who have more knowledge or experience than you.

Living in service to God is a lifelong commitment. It requires dedication, patience, and a willingness to learn and grow. With the right attitude and the right tools, however, it is possible to live a life devoted to the Lord and His teachings.

How-to live-in service to glorify God

1. Love the Lord your God with all your heart, soul, and mind. (Matthew 22:37)
2. Follow God's commands. (Deuteronomy 11:1)
3. Pray often. (1 Thessalonians 5:17)
4. Put others before yourself. (Philippians 2:3)
5. Rely on God's strength. (Isaiah 41:10)
6. Share the gospel with others. (Matthew 28:19)
7. Worship God. (John 4:24)
8. Be thankful. (1 Thessalonians 5:18)
9. Examine your heart. (Psalm 26:2)
10. Let the Holy Spirit guide your life. (Romans 8:14)

Chapter 5

Transforming Anger

We are all human, and it is natural for us to experience anger and frustration at times. However, it is important to be mindful of how we express our anger and how it impacts our lives and the lives of those around us. The Bible offers us many scriptures that can help us to transform our anger and use it to serve God instead. The Bible tells us that God is a God of love and compassion, and He desires for us to turn away from our anger and instead focus on Him and His will for us. Ephesians 4:26-27 says, "*Be angry and do not sin; do not let the sun go down on your anger, and give no opportunity to the devil.*" This scripture reminds us that it is not only possible to turn away from our anger, but that it is also necessary. When we choose to turn away from our anger and direct our focus to God, we are able to better serve Him.

Another passage in the Bible that can help us to transform our anger into serving God is James 1:19-20, which says, "*Know this, my beloved brothers: let every person be quick to hear, slow to speak, slow to anger; for the anger of man does not produce the righteousness of God.*" This scripture encourages us to be mindful of how we respond to difficult situations and to think before we speak or act. When we take our time to consider our words and actions, it is much easier to choose to serve God instead of lashing out in anger. In addition to turning away from our anger, the Bible also encourages us to forgive those who have wronged us. Matthew 6:14-15 says, "*For if you forgive others their trespasses, your heavenly Father will also forgive you, but if you do not forgive others their trespasses, neither will your Father forgive your trespasses.*" This scripture reminds us that it is not only important to forgive others, but also to forgive ourselves. When we forgive, we are able to move on from our anger and serve God instead. Finally, the Bible tells us to be thankful for the blessings in our lives.

Colossians 3:15 says, "*And let the peace of Christ rule in your hearts, to which indeed you were called in one body. And be thankful*." This scripture reminds us that when we take the time to appreciate the good in our lives, it is much easier to turn away from our anger and serve God. We all experience anger at times, but it is important to remember that we can use our anger to serve God instead of letting it control us. By turning away from our anger and focusing on God and His will for us, we can use our anger to serve Him in a powerful way. With the help of these Bible scriptures, we can be empowered to transform our anger and serve God instead.

How can I transform from my anger to pleasing God?

Read and meditate on the following scriptures and practice how to transform your anger, you will see God working marvelously in you:

1. "*Be still before the Lord and wait patiently for him; do not fret when people succeed in their ways, when they carry out their wicked schemes.*" (Psalm 37:7)
2. "*A gentle answer turns away wrath, but a harsh word stirs up anger.*" (Proverbs 15:1)
3. "*Whoever is slow to anger has great understanding, but he who has a hasty temper exalts folly.*" (Proverbs 14:29)
4. "*Cease from anger, and forsake wrath; do not fret—it only causes harm.*" (Psalm 37:8)
5. "*A man of great anger will bear the penalty, for if you rescue him, you will only have to do it again.*" (Proverbs 19:19)
6. "*Do not be quickly provoked in your spirit, for anger resides in the lap of fools.*" (Ecclesiastes 7:9)

7. "*Do not let the sun go down while you are still angry, and do not give the devil a foothold.*" (Ephesians 4:26-27)

8. "*Do all things without grumbling or disputing; that you may be blameless and innocent, children of God without blemish in the midst of a crooked and twisted generation, among whom you shine as lights in the world, holding fast to the word of life.*" (Philippians 2:14-16)

9. "*But the fruit of the Spirit is love, joy, peace, patience, kindness, goodness, faithfulness, gentleness, self-control; against such things, there is no law.*" (Galatians 5:22-23)

10. "*Be angry and do not sin; do not let the sun go down on your anger.*" (Ephesians 4:26)

Chapter 6

Moving to Forgiveness

Forgiveness is often seen as a difficult and daunting task, especially when it comes to asking for forgiveness from God. We may feel betrayed, angry, hurt, and confused. We may even feel like we're not worthy of being forgiven. But the truth is, God is more than willing to forgive us for our wrongdoings. He is always ready to receive us back into His loving embrace. The Bible tells us that God is a loving and forgiving God. He loves us so much that He sent His son Jesus to die for our sins. We know that Jesus died so that we can be forgiven and reconciled to God. He took the punishment for our sins so that we could be saved and have an eternal relationship with God. Moving to forgiveness with God starts with accepting Jesus as our Savior and Lord. We must confess our sins and ask for God's forgiveness. We must also surrender our lives to Him and trust Him to lead us to a life of righteousness.

As we surrender our lives to Him, we will begin to experience God's love, joy, peace, and forgiveness. Another important step in moving to forgiveness with God is to forgive ourselves. We must acknowledge our faults and accept that we have done wrong. We must also be willing to forgive ourselves and move forward in faith. We must recognize that God has forgiven us and He is still there for us, no matter what. Finally, we must be willing to forgive others. This can be a difficult task, especially when those who have wronged us refuse to apologize or seek forgiveness. We must understand that, even in the midst of our hurt and anger, God still loves us and is still willing to forgive us. We must also be willing to forgive others, no matter what they did to us, in order to experience true freedom and joy in our relationship with God. Forgiveness with God is a journey that requires patience and commitment. We must trust God and follow His leading as we move closer to Him. We must be willing to forgive ourselves, forgive others, and accept God's forgiveness. As we take these steps, we will experience the true freedom and joy that comes from being reconciled with God.

How do I move to forgive?

Read and meditate on the following scriptures and practice forgiving others and yourself, you will definitely become free indeed:

1. "*For if you forgive other people when they sin against you, your heavenly Father will also forgive you. But if you do not forgive others their sins, your Father will not forgive your sins*" (Matthew 6:14-15).
2. "*Blessed are the merciful, for they will receive mercy*" (Matthew 5:7).
3. "*Be kind and compassionate to one another, forgiving each other, just as in Christ God forgave you*" (Ephesians 4:32).
4. "*Therefore, as God's chosen people, holy and beloved, clothe yourselves with compassion, kindness, humility, gentleness, and patience*" (Colossians 3:12).
5. "*But if anyone does not have them [love, joy, peace, patience, kindness, goodness, faithfulness, gentleness and self control], he is nearsighted and blind, and has forgotten that he has been cleansed from his past sins*" (2 Peter 1:9).

6. "*Bear with each other and forgive one another if any of you has a grievance against someone. Forgive as the Lord forgave you*" (Colossians 3:13).
7. "*Therefore, confess your sins to one another and pray for one another, that you may be healed. The prayer of a righteous person has great power as it is working*" (James 5:16).
8. "*If we confess our sins, he is faithful and just and will forgive us our sins and purify us from all unrighteousness*" (1 John 1:9).
9. "*For I will forgive their wickedness and will remember their sins no more*" (Jeremiah 31:34).
10. "*But go and learn what this means: 'I desire mercy, not sacrifice.' For I have not come to call the righteous, but sinners*" (Matthew 9:13).

Chapter 7

Nurturing a Sense of Peace

The path to a meaningful relationship with God can often be difficult, but with patience and dedication, it is possible to nurture a sense of peace with God through the power of the Bible. The Bible is filled with scriptures that can bring comfort and peace to our souls, in times of worry and fear. By studying and exploring these scriptures, we can learn how to better connect with God and develop a sense of peace in our lives. The most important step in nurturing a sense of peace with God is prayer. We can communicate with God in the same way that we would with a friend. We can express our worries, fears, frustrations, and joys to Him, and He will listen. Prayer is an essential part of our relationship with God, as it helps us to focus our thoughts and brings us closer to Him. Reading the Bible is also essential in developing a sense of peace with God. Through reading His word, we learn about His will for our lives, and how He can help us to live in harmony with Him.

The Bible contains many passages that can bring us comfort, as well as provide us with guidance and direction. One of the most comforting Bible verses is Philippians 4:6-7, which reads "*Do not be anxious about anything, but in every situation, by prayer and petition, with thanksgiving, present your requests to God. And the peace of God, which transcends all understanding, will guard your hearts and your minds in Christ Jesus*." This passage teaches us that when we are worried, we can turn our worries over to God and find peace in Him. Another passage that can bring peace and comfort is Psalm 23:4, which reads "*Even though I walk through the valley of the shadow of death, I will fear no evil, for you are with me.*" This verse reminds us that no matter what difficulty we face in life, God is always with us, and we have nothing to fear. Finally, we can nurture a sense of peace with God by meditating on His word. We can take time out of our day to sit in silence and reflect on scripture, allowing it to sink into our hearts and minds.

We can also use Scripture to guide our daily thoughts and actions, reminding us to stay focused on God's plans for us. Nurturing a sense of peace with God is an ongoing process, but with patience and dedication, it is possible to build a strong and meaningful relationship with Him. By using the power of prayer, reading the Bible, and meditating on His word, we can grow closer to God and find comfort and peace in His presence.

How can I nurture a sense of peace in serving God?

1. Pray - Praying is one of the best ways to nurture a sense of peace with God. Philippians 4:6-7 states, "*Do not be anxious about anything, but in every situation, by prayer and petition, with thanksgiving, present your requests to God. And the peace of God, which transcends all understanding, will guard your hearts and your minds in Christ Jesus.*" Pray about your problems, fears, and troubles, and ask for God's peace to surround you.
2. Meditate on God's Word - Take time to read and meditate on Scripture. God's Word is a source of comfort and peace, and as you read, allow the Holy Spirit to speak to you through the Scripture. Psalm 119:165 says, "*Great peace have those who love your law, and nothing can make them stumble.*"
3. Practice Gratitude - Thankfulness and praise are powerful tools for connecting with God and nurturing a sense of peace. Give thanks for all the blessings God has given you, and find peace in knowing that He is watching over you. 1 Thessalonians 5:18 says, "*Give thanks in all circumstances; for this is God's will for you in Christ Jesus.*"

4. Worship – "*The Lord is near to all who call upon Him, to all who call upon Him in truth. He will fulfill the desire of those who fear Him; He also will hear their cry and save them.*" (Psalm 145:18-19)

5. Spend Time in Silence – "*Be still, and know that I am God; I will be exalted among the nations, I will be exalted in the earth!*" (Psalm 46:10)

6. Rely on His Strength – "*I can do all things through Christ who strengthens me.*" (Philippians 4:13)

7. Ask for His Guidance – "*Trust in the Lord with all your heart, and lean not on your own understanding; in all your ways acknowledge Him, and He shall direct your paths.*" (Proverbs 3:5-6)

8. Remember His Promises – "*Fear not, for I am with you; be not dismayed, for I am your God. I will strengthen you, yes, I will help you, I will uphold you with My righteous right hand.*" (Isaiah 41:10)

9. Seek Forgiveness – "*If we confess our sins, He is faithful and just to forgive us our sins and to cleanse us from all unrighteousness.*" (1 John 1:9)

10. Spend Time with Other Believers - Surrounding yourself with other believers can help you to stay focused on God and to experience peace in His presence. Hebrews 10:24-25 says, "*And let us consider how we may spur one another on toward love and good deeds, not giving up meeting together, as some are in the habit of doing, but encouraging one another and all the more as you see the day approaching.*"

Conclusion

A Prayerful Path to Peace is an invaluable guide for those seeking a path to peace and spiritual growth. It is a resource that can help one find a way to peace and harmony in the midst of a chaotic world. This book is a must-read for anyone looking to cultivate a deeper connection with their faith, and discover a new perspective on peace, love, and understanding. The journey of spiritual growth is a lifelong endeavor and the path to peace is a journey we all must take. A Prayerful Path to Peace is a valuable resource for anyone looking to deepen their spiritual practice and gain insight into the power of prayer. As we approach the New Year, let us all remain open and receptive to the power of prayer, and the potential it has to bring us closer to our desired destination of peace and contentment. May we all find the courage to take a step forward on the path to peace and create a life of love and joy.

www.ingramcontent.com/pod-product-compliance
Lightning Source LLC
LaVergne TN
LVHW052111160826
845678LV00015B/3484

9798370965586